A HASSLED GUY'S GUIDE

How to Deal

Jim Gallagher

JASMINE HEALTH

Wellness • Diet • Cooking

CHAPTER ONE

What Is Conflict?

All of the students in Mr. Ziff's tenth-grade English class are working on a group project related to the play Romeo and Juliet. The members of one group—Marco, Dan, Donald, and Melissa—cannot agree on how to do the assignment. Marco wants the group to rewrite a scene from the play so that it is set in modern times, and then act it out in class. However, Dan and Donald would prefer to write a report they can hand in. Melissa doesn't really like either idea.

Marco, Dan, Donald, and Melissa have a conflict. A conflict is what happens when there is a disagreement over two or more ideas, needs, desires, feelings, or expectations. In this case, the four students must figure out how they can work out their differences and do a good job on their project.

Everyone experiences conflict at one time or another. It is a normal part of life. But conflicts can become problems when they are not resolved in healthy ways. If people do not discuss and work out their differences, they can become tense, angry, and frustrated. In some cases, conflicts can even lead to violence.

When you are in your early teens—a time when you are experiencing a jumble of emotions and powerful new feelings—conflict can be very difficult to manage. Sometimes, young people can feel so overwhelmed by pressure that they make some bad choices. For example, they try to escape from their problems by engaging in dangerous or harmful behaviors, such as drug or alcohol abuse. Some even have thoughts of suicide.

The good news is that you can learn the skills to manage or resolve conflicts in a healthy way. Learning how to handle conflict takes practice and training, but the skills involved are important and can be used throughout your life.

"The greatest conflicts are not between two people but between one person and himself."
—Garth Brooks

Conflicts Can Occur...

- **in your personal relationships:** with family, friends, and teachers
- **in society:** among people with different values or religions, or from different ethnic groups
- **within yourself:** when you have to make a hard decision or you learn something different from your previous beliefs

CHAPTER TWO

How Conflict Makes You Feel

During a soccer game, Jeff's shot on goal smashed right into Carlos's face. As Carlos staggered back, Jeff let out a laugh. "What's so funny?" Carlos snapped. "That hurt!"

"What? Can't you take it?" snorted Jeff, as he scooped up the ball.

His heart pounding, Carlos glared at his opponent. His face was bright red—both from the impact of the ball and from anger. His hands tensed into fists.

Perhaps the reason that most people think of conflict in negative terms is because it can be a very unpleasant experience. When a disagreement starts, you suddenly experience a rush of strong feelings—your emotions. The most common emotion associated with conflict is anger. However, other feelings may include disgust, contempt, fear, anxiety, shame, guilt, and sadness.

Anger is a powerful emotion that can have a wide range of intensities. You might say that you are angry when you are merely irritated about something. But you use the same word to describe being furious and in a rage. Disgust and contempt are two emotions that often accompany feelings of anger. Disgust refers to feelings of horrified distaste for something or someone. Contempt is a feeling that someone is inferior or does not deserve respect.

You and Your Emotions

A part of everyone's personality, emotions are a powerful driving force in life. They are hard to define and understand. But what is known is that emotions—which include anger, fear, love, joy, jealousy, and hate—are a normal part of the human system. They are responses to situations and events that trigger bodily changes, motivating you to take some kind of action.

Some studies show that the brain relies more on emotions than on intellect in learning and in making decisions. Being able to identify and understand the emotions in yourself and in others can help you in your relationships with family, friends, and others throughout your life.

If you are in a conflict that lasts for a long period of time, you may also experience emotions of fear and anxiety over real or imagined danger. For example, worry and fear resulting from being teased and bullied at school can make some people become physically ill with intense headaches and overpowering nausea.

Two other emotions, shame and guilt, are also linked to conflicts, although they are rarely present during the heat of an argument. If you lose your cool during a disagreement, you may feel embarrassed afterward. This is especially true if people you like and respect witnessed your angry outburst. You may also feel guilty about having hurt a friend verbally or physically during a fight. These feelings can lead to feeling another powerful emotion—sadness—for your role in the conflict.

The mixture of emotions that accompany conflict can have a physical impact. Obviously, if you get into an argument that turns into a fistfight, you can get hurt. But conflicts that do not involve punching or other violence can cause physical changes in the body. After an unpleasant disagreement, you might feel exhausted or weak afterward. Conflict causes some teens to get headaches or stomachaches, and others to feel dizzy or lightheaded. Other symptoms related to problems with conflict are having trouble sleeping, difficulty concentrating, and worrying.

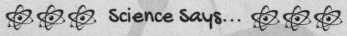 Science Says...

When you feel certain emotions, the body often responds in specific ways.

Anger and fear: increased heartbeat and an involuntary tensing of muscles

Shame: facial blushing and warmth in the upper chest or face

Sadness: tears, tightness in the throat, and heaviness in the limbs

CHAPTER THREE

Finding Solutions

> Recently, fifteen-year-old Cody has been fighting a lot with his parents. Cody's parents have been giving him a hard time about his clothes—he always wears a black shirt, jeans, and jacket. They criticize his hair, which is long and shaggy and often covers his eyes. Cody's parents complain that he and his friends seem to spend all of their time on their skateboards.
>
> Cody is a B student and has never been in trouble at school or with the law. He doesn't understand why his parents need to say anything about how he dresses or how he spends his time.

Although all conflicts are different, they share three basic elements—issues, strategies, and outcomes. Issues are the reasons that a conflict occurs. For example, one issue causing problems between Cody and his parents is his desire to be seen as an individual, while his parents wish their son were more clean-cut.

Many different kinds of issues cause conflict. People who feel threatened may want to protect themselves, their possessions, or things they respect. Conflict can occur when people hold opinions and beliefs that differ with those of others. People who believe very strongly in something generally feel that those who disagree with them are wrong.

Good and Not-So-Good Strategies Guys Use in Conflicts

1. Fight, kick, punch, push
2. Argue, curse, call each other names
3. Give the silent treatment
4. Make threats
5. Spread rumors
6. Talk it out
7. Apologize
8. Go to a teacher or another adult
9. Walk away
10. Ignore it

Naomi Drew, *The Kids Guide to Working Out Conflicts: How to Keep Cool, Stay Safe, and Get Along* (2004)

A Hassled Guy's Guide: How to Deal

Sometimes, conflict occurs just because someone looks or acts differently from others in the neighborhood. Strangers who wear unusual clothes or speak with a foreign accent may be viewed with alarm. Conflicts can occur because of ethnic, racial, or religious differences as well.

The ways that people react to and deal with conflict are called strategies. Some strategies used by teens might include fighting, talking over problems, or telling an adult.

The third element of a conflict is its result, or outcome. It is determined by the strategies a person uses to resolve the problem. According to researchers Hildy S. Ross and Cheryl L. Conant in *Conflict in Child and Adolescent Development* (1992), with every conflict, there are four possible outcomes:

1. No solution. Sometimes, the issue will simply be dropped. Cody's parents may stop hassling him about his appearance, for example. However, nothing is solved. And there is no guarantee that the issue will not arise again.

2. Giving in. Cody could give in and do what his parents want. By submitting to their wishes, he is making a conscious decision to let go of the argument. He may think, "Right now, my parents make the rules. To avoid conflict, I'll obey them. After all, I'll be on my own soon." By giving in to his parents' wishes to make them happy, Cody is giving his parents a high level of control over his life. And he most likely feels frustrated. This frustration may grow into feelings of resentment and anger that would make future conflicts with his parents more likely.

3. An adult-imposed solution. This outcome is essentially the same as giving in, but it occurs because Cody's parents have forced their son to obey their wishes. As with the giving in outcome, Cody's resentment over being forced to change would make the situation unpleasant for everyone.

4. A solution acceptable to both sides. Both Cody and his parents would have to discuss the issue

The "Win-Win" Approach

When people agree to work together to find a solution that works for everyone, they are using a "win-win" approach. In a win-win approach, both sides are encouraged to work as partners instead of opponents. Instead of each side attacking the other to try to gain an advantage, they try to come up with a solution that is fair to both parties. Compromise, bargaining, and seeking alternatives are the key components to achieving a win-win outcome.

and agree on a compromise that each can be happy with. This outcome has the best chance of long-term success. If both parties believe they are getting something they want from the solution, both will be able to support it.

Of the four possible outcomes to conflict, a solution that is acceptable to both sides is usually best. However, it can also be the most difficult one to achieve. To reach an agreement, all parties involved in the conflict must treat others with respect and work together to understand the problem and determine a solution.

Effective Communication

"You can have my science book. I'll see if I can get another copy."

"You idiot! What are you doing? That's my book! Give it back!"

"I don't like it that you took my science book without asking, but we can share during class until you replace your old one."

These three responses to a potential conflict reflect the three main styles of communication: passive, aggressive, and assertive. Depending on how you deal with a conflict, you may use all three of these styles.

People who are passive communicators try to avoid conflict with others by giving in to them. They may say things like "I don't know" or "Whatever you think is fine." Passive communicators may be afraid of making someone else uncomfortable or unhappy. However, by always putting others' needs ahead of their own,

"The strong man is the man who can stand up for his rights and not hit back. "
—Dr. Martin Luther King, Jr.

they invite others to take advantage of them. While they may head off a conflict, they may feel unhappy because their needs are not being met.

By contrast, aggressive communicators always "look out for number one." They seem to believe that others are not as important as they are. They may intentionally take advantage of, hurt, humiliate, or put down others. The aggressive communicator says things like, "Can't you see that my way is best?" or "Your idea is stupid and will never work." With their brash verbal attacks, aggressive communicators are more likely to start fights or make conflicts worse.

The way you communicate with others can affect whether conflict occurs and whether a conflict is resolved or gets worse. There is really no "right" way to communicate. Sometimes, the passive approach works best, and, other times, an aggressive approach is necessary. However, an assertive communication style is usually fair for all concerned.

Assertive communicators know their rights and express their needs and feelings honestly. They insist on being treated fairly. However, at the same time, assertive communicators also try to respect and understand others' rights, needs, and feelings. An assertive communicator is willing to cooperate to find a win-win solution.

You can't be an assertive communicator without first being a good listener. In order to be a good listener, you need to focus on what the other person is saying. If all you are thinking about is what you're going to say in response, then you are not really listening—you're preparing for an argument. If you're in the middle of doing something, stop and pay attention while the person is speaking.

An assertive communicator responds during arguments with statements like "I understand that this is important to you. It is also important to me. Instead of calling each other names, let's work together and solve the problem."

Communication Blockers

Interrupting. If you keep butting in when your friend is trying to talk, how can you hear what he has to say? This frustrating blocker is perhaps the most common communication problem.

Advising. By giving unsolicited advice, you are saying to your friend, "I know better than you do." It's better to just listen to what he has to say, and wait until he asks your opinion.

Challenging, accusing, or contradicting. These argumentative behaviors will force your friend to become defensive. Chances are, instead of resolving the fight, you will just begin a new one.

Criticizing, name-calling, or putting-down. Your friend will feel unimportant if you constantly make sarcastic, negative comments while he is talking. Why would he want to continue such a conversation?

What Is Your Communication Style?

Read the following questions, and select the **A, B,** or **C** answer that is closest to the way you honestly think you would respond to each scenario.

1. **While standing in line for tickets at a baseball game, a person ahead of you invites his friend to join him in line. You say:**

   A. "Oh, well, there's nothing I can do about it."

   B. "Hey you! Get back to the end of the line!"

   C. "When you jump ahead in line, it's not fair to the rest of us."

2. **Your English teacher says that the writing assignment you have submitted is not acceptable and that it must be redone. You reply:**

   A. "I'm an idiot and I never get anything right."

   B. "No way, that's unfair!"

   C. "Okay, but can you explain it again so I can understand what you are looking for?"

3. **Something is bothering your friend, and every time you see him he complains about it. Eventually, you start to wish he would talk about something else. The next time he brings up the subject, you say:**

   A. "Sure, sure, I understand. Go ahead and talk about what's bothering you."

   B. "Just get over it already! You're really becoming a bore."

   C. "Hey, I understand this has been bothering you, but can you think of something to do about it? I'd be happy to help if I can."

A Hassled Guy's Guide: How to Deal

4. **In the cafeteria, you put your books on a chair and go to get lunch. When you return with your tray, someone is about to move your books and sit down. Your response is:**

   A. "Oh, well, I guess I'll find somewhere else to sit."

   B. "Get your hands off my stuff, you creep!"

   C. "Excuse me, but that's my seat. There's an empty seat across the table if you'd like to sit down with us."

5. **A friend is angry because both of you have invited the same girl, Tracy, out on a date. When he confronts you, you say:**

   A. "Sorry about that. I can find someone else to ask out."

   B. "Why would Tracy want to go out with you, you jerk?"

   C. "It's up to Tracy who she goes out with. I have the right to ask her if I want to."

6. **At a store's checkout counter, you realize that the cashier did not give you the correct change. You tell her about it, but she denies making a mistake. You respond:**

   A. "Well, maybe I miscounted. Sorry to bother you."

   B. "Stop lying and give me my money right now, you thief!"

   C. "Look, I'm sure about this. Count the change yourself."

If your answers are mostly **As**, *then your usual communication style is passive. Mostly* **Bs** *means that you react aggressively to conflict. Mostly* **Cs** *means your preferred communication style is assertive.*

David Cowan, Susanna Palomares, and Dianne Schilling, *Conflict Resolution Skills for Teens* (1994)

Tips for Being a Good Listener

1. Face the speaker and look into his or her eyes.
2. Be relaxed, but pay close attention.
3. As the person speaks, try to feel what he or she is feeling.
4. Don't interrupt.
5. Let the speaker know you are listening by nodding or saying "uh huh."
6. If you don't understand something, wait until the speaker pauses and then ask him or her to explain. ("What do you mean by...?")
7. Keep an open mind.

Have your conversation in a quiet place where neither of you will be distracted. It may be hard, but control your emotions and let the other person finish speaking instead of interrupting. Allow the person who is speaking as much time as necessary to explain his or her feelings and actions.

When the speaker has finished, you should be able to repeat back, in your own words, his or her complaint. You may not agree with what was said, but if you can repeat the main idea, you will show that you were listening and trying to understand.

CHAPTER FIVE

Solving Conflicts With Friends

Chris borrowed Nick's favorite video game three months ago and didn't return it until last Friday. That night, Nick had Chris and several other friends over to his home. He was looking forward to playing the game with them, but it wouldn't work. Nick realized the disk had several deep scratches on it. Frowning, he looked at Chris.

"I paid for this game with my own money, and it cost a lot," Nick said. "You better buy me a new one."

"No, " Chris replied. "It worked okay for me. I didn't break it."

"You're lying," Nick insisted. Chris glared at his friend. Then, without saying another word, he stood up and walked out of the house.

Fighting between friends can be very painful, leaving both people feeling a mixture of emotions. Conflict can cause feelings of hurt, betrayal, anger, frustration, and sadness. This was the case with Nick. After Chris left, he felt bad about calling his friend a liar. But he was angry about his broken game. When Nick saw Chris at school the following Monday, he didn't speak to him. The silent treatment lasted a week, until Nick decided he had to do something. He still wanted to be friends with Chris.

Solving a conflict is a little like solving a math problem—you can't find the solution until you understand the problem. So your first step is to understand what the conflict is all about. Try to calmly evaluate what happened and how your friend's actions made you feel. Ask yourself, is this really important to me? Should I be angry? At the same time, try to understand how your friend feels about what happened. What would it take to resolve your conflict? What would be the most effective way?

Guys' Top Five Conflict Starters Between Friends

1. Who's right and who's wrong
2. Bragging
3. Who does better at sports or in school
4. The rules of games
5. Insults and name-calling

Naomi Drew, *The Kids Guide to Working Out Conflicts: How to Keep Cool, Stay Safe, and Get Along* (2004)

The second step—talking things over with the other person—is harder. You may find it difficult to speak with your friend after a fight because you feel embarrassed that the fight occurred in the first place. He or she may feel the same way. In addition, trying to patch things up can sometimes cause another fight. Beginning the conversation with statements like "You really made me mad last Friday" or "This problem is all your fault" will only make the other person defensive.

One way to prevent further conflict is to share your feelings without attacking or blaming the other person. Instead, you can use carefully worded statements called I-messages.

An I-message has four basic parts:

- "I feel..."

  (States how you feel about the issue that caused the conflict.)

- "...when..."

  (Gives details about what the other person did or said that caused the hard feelings.)

- "...because..."

  (Explains why you feel that way. This can be the hardest part of the I-message.)

- "I want..."

  (Describes what you think will resolve the conflict or ease the bad feelings.)

The Rules of Friendship

Pull your own weight. If one person is always giving in a friendship, the relationship is unbalanced. Support your friend, and expect that person to be there for you as well.

Don't betray a confidence. Trust is an important part of friendship. If your friend tells you a secret, don't tell others.

Beware of criticism. If a friend asks for your opinion, be honest. It is okay to tell a friend when you think he or she is making a mistake. But before you criticize your friend, think about your reasons. Do you mean well, or are you feeling envious?

Acknowledge your friend's success. You may become jealous when your friend wins the wrestling tournament while you were eliminated in the first round. But a strong person can put that jealousy aside and celebrate his friend's success.

Adapted from Florence Isaacs, *Toxic Friends, True Friends: How Your Friends Can Make or Break Your Health, Happiness, Family, and Career* (1999)

Nick decided to use I-messages the next time he saw Chris at school. "You know," Nick said, "I felt really bad last Friday when the game didn't work because I knew you were the last person to use it. But I want to talk about what happened and try to work things out."

Nick's statement addressed the fact that there was a problem but did not place blame for the fight on Chris. Nick also did not blame himself for the fight. Instead, he acknowledged that there was a problem and invited his friend to help develop a solution. He also made sure to focus on listening to what Chris had to say.

Chris was able to respond with his own I-message. "I felt angry when you assumed the broken game was my fault because I knew it wasn't. I saw your little brother throwing the disk around earlier and didn't have a chance to mention it. I felt bad that you called me a liar."

When it was Nick's turn to speak, he restated in his own words what Chris had said. Nick was paraphrasing. This is an active listening strategy—a technique that a person can use in order to hear and fully understand what another person wants. When you paraphrase, you reword and repeat what someone has just told you. "So, it sounds like I should have given you a chance to explain," Nick admitted.

After you understand where the other person is coming from, you can work together to come up with a solution to a conflict. One way to do this is by brainstorming. That is, you and the other person list all the possible solutions to your conflict. Then determine a solution you agree on.

Both Nick and Chris valued their friendship and wanted it to continue, so they had a fairly easy time coming up with a solution. Nick apologized for hurting his friend's feelings. Chris apologized for taking so long to return the game. He suggested that they share the cost of another copy so it wouldn't cost as much to replace.

Not all conflicts among friends are solved as easy as the one between Nick and Chris. Some disagreements may never be fully resolved. This does not have to mean the end of the friendship, although that sometimes happens. However, especially when a conflict is over a minor issue, two people who like and respect each other can "agree to disagree."

CHAPTER SIX

When the Group Gets Mad

Sometimes conflicts will involve more than two people. You may find yourself pulled in several directions if some of your friends don't like or get along with each other. Although conflicts involving a group may seem more complex and harder to solve than fights between two friends, you can use the exact same process to resolve disagreements. The first thing to do is to determine what the conflict is about. Is this problem basically a disagreement between two people, while others in the group have taken sides? Are a few people ganging up on someone for some reason? Are you involved because a friend expects you to take a side? Or does this conflict affect you directly?

If you find that you are at the center of a group fight, don't take sides. Instead, try to encourage everyone else to work things out. To do this, you need to determine who is directly involved. Then, spend some time alone with that person—or those people—

Steps to Solving Group Problems

Stop all blaming. Remember, blaming someone (or even yourself) for a problem will not solve it.

Define the problem. Ask yourself two questions: "What is the problem?" and "Whose problem is it?" If it is not your problem, let the person who "owns" the problem solve it.

Consider asking for help. Once you have thought about the problem, you may want to talk things over with someone else, such as another friend or a trusted adult.

Think of alternative solutions. Brainstorm to come up with as many possible ideas for solving the problem as you can.

Evaluate the alternatives. To determine the best approach, think carefully about how each possible solution will affect you and others.

Make a decision. Choose the alternative that you believe is most likely to succeed and least likely to hurt anyone.

Follow through. Once you've made a decision, stick to it. However, if after a reasonable amount of time you find things aren't working, try an alternative solution.

Adapted from David Cowan, Susanna Palomares, and Dianne Schilling, *Conflict Resolution Skills for Teens* (1994) and talk about what's going on. Listen carefully to figure out what the problem is. Then, explain that you both should brainstorm together to find a solution.

There are some times, however, when you have to take sides in a group conflict, such as when it involves dangerous or illegal activities. For example, a friend in your group may be using drugs or encouraging others to shoplift. In such cases, you need to be true to yourself and what you believe in. Confront your friend, and explain that what he or she is doing is wrong—and dangerous.

If your friend ignores you, then it is time to tell a parent, teacher, or another trusted adult. This can be very hard—your friend will get into trouble, and you will probably lose his or her trust. But you need to do the right thing. If others in your group are also concerned, ask them to join you when talking to your friend. If necessary, go as a group to tell an adult about the problem.

Even if the group conflict does not involve a serious issue, if the fighting drags on for a long time, it's okay to ask an adult to help resolve the problem. School counselors and teachers usually have had a lot of experience helping groups of kids resolve conflicts and fights just like yours. You might also talk to a parent or to some other trusted adult.

CHAPTER SEVEN

"Quit Picking on Me!"

Since the beginning of the school year, Jesse has been bullied in gym class by two larger guys. They constantly tease him, throw his books and papers into the shower, and slap and punch him when no one is looking. Jesse has been too afraid to do anything about it.

Bullying **can be physical assaults or verbal abuse—or both.** There are many reasons why bullying occurs. Some kids feel a sense of power and control when teasing or harassing their classmates. Others act out as a way to get the attention of their peers. Still others bully to compensate for feelings of inadequacy. They target classmates as a way of venting frustration with problems at home or in school. Some people bully because they've been bullied themselves.

Bullies usually torment peers who are weak, unpopular, and unlikely to resist. They often focus on those who are different in some way. Targets can be the new kid who wears the "wrong" clothes, the "teacher's pet," the student with a speech defect or

What to Do If You Are Being Bullied

1. Unless you believe you may be physically harmed, confront your tormentor. Look the bully in the eye and tell him, firmly and clearly, to stop.

2. Get away from the situation as quickly as possible.

3. Tell an adult what has happened immediately. If you are afraid to tell a teacher on your own, ask a friend to go with you.

4. Keep on speaking up until you get someone to listen. Explain what happened, who was involved, where it occurred, and what you have done.

5. Remember, bullying is not your fault—don't blame yourself for what has happened.

Adapted from Dorothea M. Ross, *Childhood Bullying and Teasing: What School Personnel, Other Professionals, and Parents Can Do* (2003) learning disability, or the overweight classmate. You can be bullied in many different ways.

You may be called names, or be pushed, shoved, or hit. You may have your belongings taken or damaged, or be threatened. Bullying may involve having rumors or gossip spread about you at school or on the Internet.

Bullying is a form of conflict that causes many emotions. If you are the victim of bullying, you probably feel very angry, but also powerless. It's likely that you also feel afraid, especially if you are threatened or physically attacked. You may feel so much anxiety that you'll try to avoid the bullies at any cost: skipping school or staying away from places where you might run into them. You may also feel ashamed at not being able to stand up to the bullies.

You need to recognize that you are not at fault. It is the other person who is behaving in an unacceptable way. No one deserves to be bullied. However, if you are constantly fighting with others or hearing a lot of negative comments from bullies, you can begin to think badly about yourself. This development of low self-esteem can lead to more serious problems, including depression and thoughts of suicide.

Low self-esteem was a problem for one guy who shared his story anonymously on the Web site *JaredStory.com*. He first encountered problems with

What to Do If You See Someone Being Bullied

Most people are uncomfortable when they see someone being bullied. They often feel guilty because they want to intervene but don't want the bully to begin targeting or tormenting them. According to i-Safe America's "Cyber Bullying: Statistics and Tips," if you see someone being bullied:

1. **Refuse to join in.** It can be hard, but do your best to resist the bully's efforts to get you to tease or torment someone.

2. **If you can, try to defuse the situation.** Try to draw attention away from the person being targeted. If you know the bully, perhaps you can take him aside and ask him to leave the victim alone. However, don't place yourself at risk.

3. **Get help.** Ask a teacher, parent, or other responsible adult to come and help immediately.

4. **Offer support to bullied teens.** Help them up if they have been tripped or knocked down. If you believe you can't do this safely at the time, give words of kindness or condolence later to those who have been hurt.

5. **Encourage the victims to talk with an adult.** Offer to go along if it would help. If the victim of a bully is unwilling to report the incident, tell an adult yourself. (If necessary for your safety, do this anonymously.)

Cyberbullying

A 2004 survey by i-Safe America of fourth through eighth graders reported that 42 percent of them said they had been bullied through the computer—by having personal information or embarrassing photographs of themselves posted online without their knowledge or permission.

Another 35 percent of students said they had been threatened in hostile instant messages or text on Web sites. More than half admitted to having said hurtful things to others online. Almost 60 percent said they did not tell their parents or any other adult about what happened.

bullying when in elementary school. Over the years, the abuse continued, and he became severely depressed. He explained, "I would stay up crying and wishing I were dead. I have tried to kill myself many times. Now I am in high school and nothing has changed. I still want to die but I go to counseling to get help."

All young people go through periods of sadness, but deep unhappiness and feelings of hopelessness and despair that last more than a week or two are considered depression. It is an emotional problem that interferes with a teen's ability to function in school and at home.

If you believe you are affected by depression, get help by talking to someone you trust—a friend, your parents, a school counselor, your family doctor, a religious leader—or call a suicide prevention hotline (see page 63). The same holds true if you have a friend who seems depressed. Without support, someone suffering from depression is in danger of hurting himself or possibly taking his own life. According to the U. S. Centers for Disease Control and Prevention, the third leading cause of death among fifteen- to twenty-five-year-olds is suicide, and 86 percent of all teenage suicides are boys.

Some of the Symptoms of Depression

- A loss of interest in activities previously enjoyed
- Feelings of worthlessness or guilt
- Fatigue or loss of energy
- Withdrawal from friends and family
- Easily annoyed and frustrated
- Sudden decline in grades
- Appetite or weight changes

CHAPTER EIGHT

Are You a Bully?

Fourteen-year-old Tucker knows how it feels to be bullied. In school, some of the bigger ninth graders pick on him at lunch. They call him names and sometimes punch him hard in the arm or shoulder. When Tucker gets home, though, he and his friends often tease an eleven-year-old neighborhood boy named Jed. They make fun of Jed's learning disability and call him mean names. "I don't know why I do it," admits Tucker, who feels somewhat guilty and ashamed. "I know how much I hate being teased at school."

Even if you are the victim of a bully, there may be times that you want to bully other kids. Like Tucker, you may not give much thought to your behavior. In fact, Tucker usually tells other people that he is not a bully. He says he is just "fooling around."

Think about how you treat other people—put yourself in their shoes. Ask yourself how you would feel if someone knocked you down or called you names. Chances are, you wouldn't feel very good about it or about yourself.

Some bullies eventually realize that their behavior is self-destructive and make an effort to change. They come to recognize that their behavior is not really making them look strong and powerful to others. Instead, it makes them appear weak—as well as mean.

If you think you have been acting like a bully and you want to stop, the first step is to talk to the person you've bullied. Apologize for your past behavior. Then, the next time you see that person, make an effort to have something good to say. To stop yourself from being a bully, you need to recognize that you are placing your own anger and other negative emotions on your victim. And that behavior is not healthy for either of you. If you think you need help to change your ways, you might want to talk to your parents or to a school counselor.

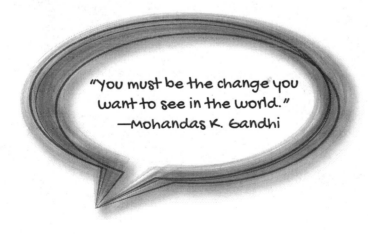

"You must be the change you want to see in the world."
—Mohandas K. Gandhi

Some Myths About Bullying

Myth #1: Bullying is just teasing.

Fact: Bullying is much more than teasing. Bullies may also use violence, threats, or other tactics. When everyone involved considers teasing to be fun, then it can be considered a joke. But bullying hurts.

Myth #2: Some people deserve to be bullied.

Fact: No one deserves to be bullied. Most bullies torment people who are "different" from them, but being different is not a reason to be bullied.

Myth #3: Bullying is a normal part of growing up.

Fact: It is not normal to be pushed around, teased, threatened, insulted, hurt, or abused.

Myth #4: People who are bullied will get over it.

Fact: Bullying hurts for a long time. Some victims of bullies drop out of school because of their fear. Some become depressed or even commit suicide. If you ask an adult, chances are he or she will remember being bullied. People don't "get over" being bullied easily.

Adapted from Pamela Espeland, *Life Lists for Teens: Tips, Steps, Hints, and How-tos for Growing Up, Getting Along, Learning, and Having Fun* (2003)

CHAPTER NINE

When Peers Help Solve Problems

Jake accidentally bumped into Shawn in the hallway, causing him to stumble and fall. "Hey, you!" Shawn yelled. "Watch where you're going, you idiot."

Jake was tired of Shawn's attitude. For the past couple of weeks, Shawn had found every opportunity to insult Jake, criticizing him and calling him names in the hallways and lunchroom and during recess. "Oh, shut up," he retorted. "No one cares what you think."

As Shawn and Jake stared angrily at each other, a crowd of students began to gather. "Hold everything," another student called out, as he stepped between the two. "Seems like you both need to go to peer mediation."

Sometimes, two people get into a disagreement that they are unable to resolve on their own. If they are lucky, their school may have a program that helps with conflicts. In peer mediation programs, students who are involved in a dispute take their problem to a neutral third party, or mediator. The peer mediator is also a student. He or she doesn't take sides in the conflict but tries to help find a win-win solution to the problem.

When two people submit their argument for peer mediation, they must agree to follow the program's ground rules and steps. Then the peer mediator works with them to define the problem. First, one person is given a chance to speak, and then the other tells his or her side of the story. The mediator can ask questions to clarify things. When they are finished, sometimes the mediator will ask each party to repeat the other's story to show that both points of view are clearly understood.

Peer Mediation Ground Rules

- Solve the problem
- Tell the truth
- Listen without interrupting
- Be respectful
- Take responsibility for carrying out the agreement
- Keep the situation private

Adapted from Teacher Talk, "Peer Mediation," School of Education, University of Indiana, June 30, 1997

The next step is for each of the parties involved to suggest ways to resolve the part of the problem that he or she is responsible for. This will show areas where each side might be willing to compromise.

Finally, both parties brainstorm possible solutions to their problem. Each solution should be discussed and evaluated. Eventually, both parties will agree to a solution (or, in some cases, a combination of solutions). This agreement must be done freely—if one person is pressured into accepting a solution, the mediation process will probably not work out.

Peer Mediation Steps

1. Agree upon the ground rules.
2. Each student tells his or her story.
3. Verify the stories.
4. Discuss the stories.
5. Generate solutions.
6. Discuss solutions.
7. Select a solution.
8. Sign a contract.

Adapted from Teacher Talk, "Peer Mediation," School of Education, University of Indiana, June 30, 1997

The agreed-upon solution is then written down as a contract, which all participants sign. It usually consists of a simple statement such as "I will stop calling Michael names if he will stop calling me names."

Today, thousands of elementary, middle, and high schools across the nation make use of peer mediation programs. School administrators believe they help reduce incidents of violence, absences, and suspensions. But such programs also provide students with the chance to talk to their peers about issues they might have a hard time bringing up with an adult.

Peer mediation is not really about deciding who is right and who is wrong in a particular argument. Instead, the process is meant to help students learn how to move beyond the immediate conflict, resolve problems peacefully, and get along better with each other.

CHAPTER TEN

Conflicts With Adults

Derek thinks his history teacher doesn't like him. Yesterday, when he left his seat to sharpen his pencil, Mrs. Spellman yelled at him and told him that he had just earned a detention. Later, when students were talking during class, she sent Derek to the principal's office. He felt the punishment wasn't fair because he wasn't the one doing most of the talking. And this wasn't the first time that he thought his teacher was punishing him for things he didn't do.

At times, everyone gets into disagreements with people who are not their peers: parents, teachers, or other adults. If you were in Derek's position, what would you do?

Well, just like you do with peer conflicts, you need to take some time and think about the cause of this particular kind of conflict. Is the teacher angry about something you are doing or because you are not trying hard in class? If so, perhaps if you change your behavior the situation will improve.

Does your teacher seem to have a personal grudge against you, or does he or she appear to treat everyone unfairly? Answer this question honestly—maybe you are being oversensitive. Teachers are human, too (believe it or not!). Just like you, they can get annoyed and angry and sometimes take out their frustration on others unfairly.

Your first step in resolving an issue with your teacher is to ask him or her if you could meet to discuss your problem. When you meet, remain calm and respectful as you outline your concerns.

If you decide that there really is a problem between you and an adult, it's probably better not to confront the adult yourself. If you accuse your teacher of hating you, saying so may make things worse instead of better.

Resolving Conflict Through Negotiation

1. Agree to negotiate.
2. Gather points of view.
3. Focus on interests.
4. Create win-win solutions.
5. Evaluate solutions.
6. Create an agreement.

Adapted from Donna Crawford and Richard Bodine, *Conflict Resolution Education: A Guide to Implementing Programs in Schools, Youth-Serving Organizations, and Community and Juvenile Justice Settings* (October 1996)

In fact, he or she may think you are the one being unfair and looking to start an argument.

Get other adults to help you—tell your parents about the situation and ask for their advice. Be honest about what is going on and tell the whole story. Your parents may have good advice on how to deal with the problem, or they may want to step in and make sure it is resolved.

In Derek's case, after he told his mother about the problem in history class, she scheduled a meeting with his teacher, Mrs. Spellman. At the meeting, Derek's mom did not accuse the teacher of mistreating her son. She simply asked to talk about the situation. Derek's mother learned that Mrs. Spellman was having a hard time with several troublemakers in her class, and that Derek was often caught in the middle. Derek's mother then scheduled a second meeting with Mrs. Spellman and a vice principal at the school. The vice principal agreed to sit in on the class; if things didn't get better, Derek would be moved to a different class.

Obviously, every conflict involving adults or non-peers will have different causes and issues. The important thing is not to panic or get angry. Many of the same strategies used to resolve conflicts with peers can be used to solve problems with family members or adults.

Differing Perspectives

As with all conflicts, the reasons for disagreements between young people and adults can vary. Poor communication and lack of respect often play a large part. Sometimes, young people do not think about how their behavior affects other people. At the same time, adults may unfairly mistrust young people or have negative attitudes toward them.

Consider, for example, the conflict that develops between a shopkeeper and a group of teenagers who spend hours at a time hanging out in front of his store. The kids are surprised and upset when the store owner tells them to leave. From their perspective, they are not bothering anyone. They are just having fun together.

The shopkeeper, however, has a different perspective. In the past, he has had problems with kids hassling customers and stealing things. Also, the group of kids is loud and boisterous, and he is worried that they may be scaring customers away.

To resolve this conflict, both sides need to meet so they can negotiate and brainstorm ideas to solve their conflict. Possible solutions? The shopkeeper could permit the teens to sit in front of his store only during certain times of the day. The kids could promise to be quieter and not block the entrance or annoy customers.

Tips for Talking to Adults

Bring up your issue when the adult has the time to listen. Don't try to talk when they're busy with something else. Say, "Is this a good time for you? I have something important to discuss."

Be aware of your body language. Don't roll your eyes, cross your arms, or clench your fists. Look the other person in the eyes and try to remain calm.

Use respectful language. Don't use sarcasm, insults, or put-downs when explaining your point of view. Snapping something like, "That's a stupid reason," will only make the other person angry.

Be honest. Tell the truth about how you feel or what has happened.

Listen to the other side of the issue. The adult will be more likely to show you the same respect.

State your case using I-messages. "I felt upset when I got detention because I wasn't talking in class. I want you to understand what really happened."

CHAPTER ELEVEN

Fighting With Your Siblings

Did you know that it is common for baby great white sharks to eat each other? When the first sharks hatch inside the mother's body, they get additional nourishment by eating most of the unhatched eggs. Of the approximately sixty eggs that the female great white produces, sometimes only two or three will be born. Somehow, the young sharks instinctively know that their best chance for survival comes by eliminating their brothers and sisters, who would otherwise compete for their food.

The word *competition* is used to describe a struggle for limited resources, such as food. It can also be used to describe a contest in which two or more people seek the same goal. Another word that is sometimes used to describe an intense competition between two people is *rivalry*. When brothers or sisters argue among themselves, it is known as sibling rivalry.

Chances are, you don't fight with your brothers to decide which of you will get to eat dinner. But most family fights do involve a limited resource—the love and attention of your parents. If one sibling feels that he or she is not getting enough attention, he or she is going to feel jealous of other family members.

You might feel jealous, for example, if your parents get very excited about something your older brother has done, such as getting good grades or winning a sports award. Even though you're probably also proud of him, you may feel hurt, particularly if you think that your parents never made an equally big fuss over something you did.

Jealousy is often accompanied by strong emotions, such as anger and frustration. Siblings often express these feelings by fighting with each other, which makes things worse. If you get in trouble for starting a fight, you're going to feel even angrier and more frustrated. Or, once the fight is over, you may feel guilty for having upset your brother or sister.

You'll feel better about yourself if you can keep your temper when you recognize that you are feeling jealous, angry, or frustrated. It may help to leave the room and think about things for a few minutes. Has your sibling really done something that should make you angry? Or are you just frustrated with the situation? You may find that you're not even really upset at your brother or sister but just want to take out your frustration on someone.

Beating the Green-Eyed Monster!

Jealousy is one of the most common emotions. It doesn't matter how old you are, or how rich and famous—everyone struggles with jealousy sometimes. Until you learn how to handle this "green-eyed monster," life is going to be pretty miserable.

To deal with feelings of jealousy, try to forget about the other person and think about yourself. That is, instead of concentrating on what your sibling has or what he or she does, think about all the things that you have and who you are. For example, you may feel jealous because your brother won a prize for his drawing, but perhaps you are better at something else: sports or math or writing. If your parents give your sister a new bike, think about the special things your parents have given to you. Chances are, your parents are not trying to favor either of you.

Feelings of jealousy may not go away until you let them out. You may want to write down what you are feeling, or talk privately with one of your parents or family members. If you try to hold in your feelings, they will eventually boil over into frustration and anger. Expressing your feelings will help your jealousy go away—at least a little bit—and you'll feel better.

Tips for Getting Along With Brothers and Sisters

Spend some time together. Invite your younger sister to play a board game with you. Ask your older brother to kick the soccer ball around. If you spend a little time together, you can understand what he or she is thinking.

Go out of your way to give your brother or sister a compliment. Positive communication is key to building a strong, healthy relationship.

Show an interest in your sibling's hobbies and interests. Attend his or her sporting events, dance recitals, and other activities. Share your own hobbies and interests, too.

Pick your battles. If your sibling did something deliberately to hurt you, then you need to confront him or her. But nothing good results from getting mad if your brother or sister broke something of yours accidentally.

If you find yourself becoming irritated over something your sibling has done, take time to cool down. Walk away from the situation. Take a deep breath and count to ten. When you can think more calmly, come back and talk things out using a calm, quiet voice.

CHAPTER TWELVE

Fighting With Your Parents

Doug had made plans to go to the movies on Saturday afternoon with his friend Kyle. But on Saturday morning, Doug's parents announced that the family was going to spend the day cleaning up the house and doing yard work. Doug was very angry. He had done his chores all week and was looking forward to time for himself. Why were his parents being so unfair?

Like Doug, you may sometimes feel like your parents' rules are unreasonable. However, when parents establish rules it is usually because they have your best interests in mind.

For many years, your parents' most important job has been watching out for you. When you were very young, your parents made almost all of the decisions that affected you—what you ate, what clothes you wore, and how you spent your time. As you grow older and become more independent, your parents may find it hard to "let go" and allow you to make your own choices. At the same time, they may be asking you to give up some of your time in order to help out at home.

One way to avoid conflict with your parents is to talk with them regularly. Tell them how you feel about their rules. And let them know your opinions. Be honest. How can your parents understand what you are thinking and feeling if you don't tell them?

If your parents establish a rule that you happen to think is unfair—a curfew, a time limit on Internet use, or a demand that you cut your hair or wear different clothes—don't scream or yell at them. You'll have better luck if you clearly and calmly explain why you feel their rule is unfair. Make sure you have their complete attention when you are talking to them. When you are finished, ask them to explain why they feel such a restriction is important or necessary, and listen carefully to their reasons. They may have good reasons that you had not considered.

If you want greater freedom, it might help to show your parents that you are willing to take on more responsibility. Perhaps together you can work out a compromise. Offer to do additional chores if they will let you go to a concert with your friends, watch a particular television program, or stay out an hour later on a Friday night.

In Doug's case, he didn't argue with his parents. He calmly explained to them that he had already made plans for the afternoon. He said that he would be happy to work around the house in the morning, and promised to do whatever work was left on Sunday afternoon. When he was finished talking, his parents agreed to let him go to the movies. They acknowledged that Doug was good about doing his chores—a sign of responsibility—and they had not known that he had already made plans.

Sometimes your parents might not be willing to compromise or change their minds. In those cases, you will have to abide by their decision, even though you feel it is unfair. But if you continue to show your parents that you are responsible, they are more likely to be willing to give you greater freedom.

Sometimes you may have a conflict over how to handle arguments your parents are having with each other. Some may be about little things, like doing chores, weekend plans, or what's for dinner. Or arguments may be about bigger things, like family finances.

When your parents disagree, you may feel worried, sad, or upset. But it's important to keep in mind that arguments usually do not mean parents don't love each other, or that they're going to get a divorce.

Everyone loses his or her temper occasionally. Even if the argument is about you, remember that it is not your fault.

Sometimes arguments can become unpleasant. Parents may yell and scream, call each other names, and say nasty things to each other. If this happens, you may feel that you have to become involved. The best approach is to wait until the shouting has ended, and your parents have cooled down. Then, talk to them individually. Without blaming anyone, tell your parents how their arguments make you feel. That thought may help them control their tempers the next time they become angry with each other.

In a few cases, arguments get out of control and parents throw things or hit each other. This type of behavior is never okay. You need to let another adult

Sources of Conflicts with Parents

- Homework
- Chores
- Curfew
- Talking back
- Report card grades
- Arguments with siblings

know what is going on. Talk to close relatives, a teacher, a school counselor, or a trusted family friend. That adult may be able to speak with your parents or help them get counseling.

Crisis Hotlines

If you believe a friend or family member is in danger because of violence at home, pick up the phone and call a crisis hotline. The number for the National Domestic Violence Hotline appears on page 63.

CHAPTER THIRTEEN

You're Not Alone

> *Trey is in his first year at a large middle school, and he doesn't know many people. Every morning during homeroom, the two guys seated behind him make mean and insulting comments about him. They're speaking too low for the teacher to hear. Derrick—the guy sitting next to Trey—is friendly most of the time. But when the guys behind Trey start teasing him, Derrick doesn't say anything. Trey doesn't want to fight or tell the teacher. He's feeling angry, frustrated, and anxious, but most of all he is feeling isolated because of this conflict.*

Trey is not alone—everyone experiences some conflict practically every day. Conflict causes stress and can damage or destroy relationships if it is not managed properly. That's why it is so important for young people to understand how to deal with the conflicts in their lives.

If you are feeling upset about a conflict, it may be helpful to remember that conflict is normal. Talk to your parents or another trusted adult—chances are, they will be able to tell you stories about conflicts or bullying that happened to them when they were your age. Ask your friends to share their stories, and you'll find that they are probably similar to yours.

The basic steps to resolving conflict are the same in all cases. First, you need to understand exactly what the issue is. Also, think about your own feelings about the conflict because that will help you to control your emotions more easily.

The next step is to address the conflict. This may involve confronting another person, but it should be

Five Things to Say When Someone Makes Fun of You

1. _____(In other words, say nothing. Just ignore it. If that doesn't work, turn and walk away.)
2. I don't like it when you tease me, and I want you to stop.
3. So?
4. Do you have a problem with that? I don't have a problem with that.
5. Thank you for noticing.

Adapted from Pamela Espeland, *Life Lists for Teens: Tips, Steps, Hints, and How-tos for Growing up, Getting Along, Learning, and Having Fun* (2003)